my DoG is a CARROT

john Hegley

For Isabella

The author would like to thank Beth Aves for the interior color coordination (the brightness within), Patrick Insole for the potato typography, and Jackie di Stefano for the carrot photography.

Copyright © 2002 by John Hegley

Selected poems taken from *Glad to Wear Glasses* by John Hegley. Copyright © 1990 by John Hegley. Reproduced by permission of Andre Deutsch Ltd.

First U.S. edition 2003

Library of Congress Cataloging-in-Publication Data is available.
Library of Congress Catalog Card Number 2002018911

ISBN 0-7636-1932-9

10 9 8 7 6 5 4 3 2 1

Printed in Hong Kong

This book was typeset in Franklin Gothic and Kosmik. The illustrations were done in felt-tip and ballpoint pen.

Candlewick Press
2067 Massachusetts Avenue
Cambridge, Massachusetts 02140

visit us at www.candlewick.com

my DoG is a CARROT

john Hegley

State Library of Ohio

SEO Library Center
40780 SR 821 * Caldwell, OH 43724

CANDLEWICK PRESS
CAMBRIDGE, MASSACHUSETTS

content

S

R

L

You can cut out these glasses and put them on: a) your face, b) your dog, or c) your cornflakes.

Me poem

me

me

me

me ME

me

Me me me

Me

me

me

me

Me

me

me

me

Me me me

Me me me me. ME me Me

Me

me

ME

me

me

ME me me me me

me me me me me me me,
that's enough about me.

my glasses are my glasses

Here are my glasses
they are brown
unless you turn
the color down.

My glasses come in two main parts
the lenses and the frame
I really like my glasses
but they haven't got a name.

Well they have
but it's just glasses,
as simple as can be
I look after my glasses
because they look after me.

I've got my glasses on my face
I've got my glasses in the proper place
but one day when I was running in a sack race
my glasses fell off onto the running track
and somebody behind me
deliberately hopped on top of them
and damaged them really badly.

Grandad's glasses

we never used to ask questions
about his glasses
he needed them to see TV
and that was that
but then one day
he couldn't see TV anymore
so he didn't need his glasses
and there was no point in burying them with him
because
a) his eyes were shut
and b) none of us believed in TV after death
we had a family get-together about it
and after the big argument
we came up with two possibilities
a) find someone with glasses like grandad's
and give them the glasses
and b) find someone with glasses like grandad's
and sell them the glasses

Grandma's glasses

my grandmother used to say
before you moan
about the muck on someone else's glasses
make sure you're not talking about the muck on your own

her glasses were filthy

Wipe wipe wipe your glasses

I've seen people with mud on their glasses
I've seen people with blood on their glasses,
once I saw a lad
who had the leg of a daddy-long-legs on his glasses.
He thought they were cracked.
But they weren't.

Poem about losing **my glasses**

the place is unfamiliar
my face is bare
I've mislaid my glasses
I've looked in my glasses case
but they're not there
and I need my glasses
to find my glasses
but I'm going to be all right
I've got a spare pair

somewhere

My doggie don't wear glasses

my doggie don't wear glasses
so they're lying when they say
a dog looks like its owner
aren't they

A comparison of logs and dogs

both are very popular at Christmas

but it is not generally considered cruel

to abandon a log

and dogs are rarely used as fuel

loggie

Pet

John was feeling a bit lonely
so he decided to pretend that his portable TV
  was a little dog.
The screen was its face
the cable was its tail
and the screws at the back
they were its fleas.
John was very happy with his new friend
until one day she became very ill
after John had given her a bath.
When the repairman came
John called out IT'S ALL RIGHT PET
THE VET'S HERE!
and he led the man into the living room
and showed him his portable TV all wrapped
  up in blankets
and the repairman took out a great big screwdriver
and pushed it into John's throat.
"Oh great," said John,
"You're going to get rid of her little fleas as well
  are you?"
The repairman thought he was teasing,
he didn't find it pleasing
and he took hold of John and he hit him
and the portable TV jumped up and bit him.

Max
(likes to be with people but people . . . .

Max is a dog with a problem
the sort of problem it's a job to ignore
the first time they all thought it was funny
but not anymore
picture the scene this home-loving hound
is sleeping by the fire with the family around
he wakes up and makes a little sound
little Albert gets it first
he's nearest to the ground
Albert's mom gets wind of it
and she says open the door
and whatever we've been feeding him
I don't think we should give him no more
Max does another one like old kippers

wakes up Daddy in his fireside slippers
Daddy wakes up and says open the door
Albert says it's open Dad I did it when he did
   it before
then Mom says it's hard to relax with Max around
yesterday it happened while we were out in the car
and it's a small car
and Granny she was sick
she's not used to it like we are
maybe we could swap him for a pet ant
Max is smelly
he can spoil it when you're watching television
but luckily
he's not an elephant

Volume, as in space

How many elephants
can you get in a car?
You can make an equation:
take the room inside the car
and divide it by the average volume of an elephant
and a more than average amount of persuasion

Books, as in libraries

My boyhood days
I spent the phase
in Luton by the Lea
and I always got a lovely vibe from Luton Libe-
   raree
four new books a borrowing
it would to me lend
and as I turned the pages
they turned into my friends
the only ones I had
according to my dad

People

Using:

Borrowing

Learning

Interneting.

Closed

   Wednesday.

Local

Information,

Books,

Records,

And

Relaxation.

Yo!

A BOY'S BEST GIFT

One day when I was seven or so

I told my dad of my desperate desire for a Christmas dog.

And he said "No no no no no no no no no **NO.**

NO!"

It didn't look too good.

"Why do you want a dog anyway?"

"Because I have no friends."

"But you've got Tony. Tony's your friend."

"Tony was my friend and then he got a dog,

now his dog's his friend."

"I'm sorry John, no dog and that's the end of it."

That Christmas my dad got me a kennel.

After the initial bewilderment

I crawled inside and became the very dog I had requested.

I became my own best friend.

RED AND BLUE POEM

Danger,

Don't tip that

strawberry jelly

into the mailbox

Stop, Stop! If the mail

truck turns up now you'll be so

embarrassed,

Dad.

Pat and the

everything seemed flat to Pat

so she sat on her bike

and cycled around to see her Uncle Matt the wizard

even though her tires were flat

and there was a blizzard

so what's the matter Pat said Matt

and Pat explained and Matt said Pat

let me look inside my hat

there's nothing there he looked and said

then put his hat back on his head

and went all red and rolled about

and spat a pair of glasses out

wizard

now look through these the wizard said

and Pat she put them on her head

and said

the world's NOT flat

Christopher Columbat

just wait until I tell my cat

she didn't know her cat was dead

splattered flat by Uncle Fred

it's lucky Uncle Matt was skilled

at mending cats his brother killed

Pat gave out a happy holler

and all he charged was fifty cents.

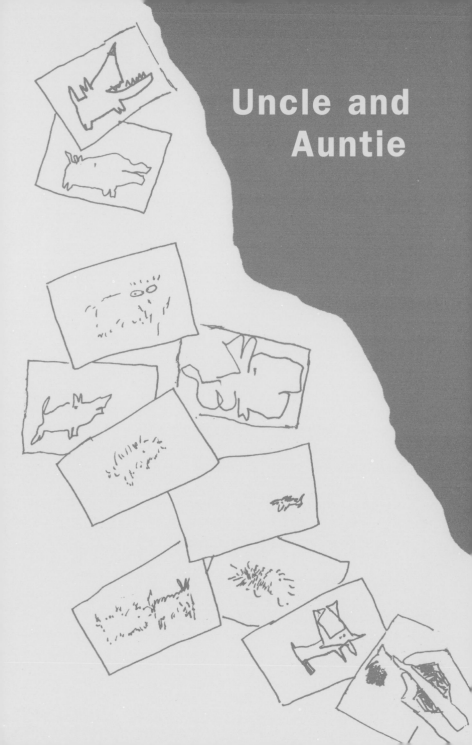

Uncle and
Auntie

my auntie gives me a coloring book and crayons
I begin to color
after a while auntie leans over and says
you've gone over the lines
what do you think they're for
eh?
some kind of statement is it?
going to be a rebel are we?
your auntie gives you a lovely present
and you have to go and ruin it
I begin to cry
my uncle gives me a hanky and some blank paper
do some doggies of your own he says
I begin to color
when I have done
he looks over
and says they are all very good
he is lying
only some of them are

Did I, Dad?

Dad,
Did I ever say how glad
I am to have you?
What about you, Mom?
No?
How dumb
How mad.

Mainly pink poem

Last
Christmas,
I got my brother-in-law
a pink sweater.
He was not happy.
When he'd torn open the wrappy
he said,
"I don't think pink is what a man should wear."
I said, "It's not off-the-shelf,
I knitted it myself."
He said, "I don't care,
and I don't think men should knit
either, but that's up to you."
I said, "At least you can put it
in Thumper's basket."
(Thumper is the dog of my brother-in-law.)
My brother-in-law said,
"Thumper won't sleep a wink
on a pink sweater.
He's a *boy* dog.
Pink is not for boy dogs, boy men, boy anythings."
I said, "What about boy ants?"
My brother-in-law said he wasn't sure about boy ants.
Then he opened the gift from my sister.
It was some women's undies.
Blue ones.

Sister, with this hand I made a fist and made it land upon your sandcastle. I am sorry. Let me make you a new one.

Poem about my sister

My dad told my sister not to play with
  her food.
It was reasonable advice,
carrots do not make very good friends.

An owner's complaint
I've got a dog that's more
like a carrot than a dog.
It's hairy,
but only very slightly.
It's got no personality
to speak of,
no bark to bark of,
no head
no legs
no tail
and it's all
orange
and
crunchy.

For the soup

There once was an organic leek
that had managed to learn how to speak,
at the sight of a knife
it would fear for its life
and go **eeeeeeeeeeeeeeeeeeeeeek!**

Limberick

There was once a woman of Gwent
who was useless at pitching a tent
she hammered a peg
through a bone in her leg
and immediately after, she went
aaaaaaaaaaaargh.

The bare BONES
of a poem

The skeleton gives flesh its shape
there isn't one inside a grape.
The skeleton is made of bone
it helps you stand up on your own.
The skeleton is strong and firm

there isn't one inside a worm.

Or a banana.

Or a potato.

Or a box of crackers.

Or a worm.

Oh no, I've said worm already.

Body poem

The human body's a machine,
the spaceship of the self,
and perfect working order means
you're in the best of health.
The brain is the computer,
the mind, a kind of screen,
the human body's a machine
that comes in many colors,
but not green.

Or anything stripey.

JEAN

Jean was keen on computer games
but not on hide-and-seek.
Jean lived in computer heaven
seven days a week.
She stayed in front of the screen until
she'd forgotten how to speak.

Bully for you

If you're being bullied,
tell.
Tell your parents
tell your guardians
tell your caregivers,
tell your home-livers
tell your teacher
tell your principal
tell your vice-principal
tell the teacher who is vice-principal
when the principal is away
and the deputy has to move up one,
tell all of them.

TELL

In class

by chance
I glance at her answer paper
protective of her labor
my next-door neighbor
drops an accusing karate chop
across the page-top
to stop me from copying
as she writes

her name

sub sobbing

The snub

at school I used to play a lot of Subbuteo
(a table football game)
and they used to call me Sub
and it was good to have a nickname
until they told me it stood for substandard

Jane and Wojtek

Wojtek was a Polish boy in my class
when I was about seven, Jane wasn't.
I fancied Jane, Jane fancied Wojtek:

when I saw Jane and Wojtek kiss
I was jealous of their bliss
and I reported them to miss

Listen

Mom and Dad, I'm feeling sad
let me tell you why,
there's a girl at school
I love up to the sky
but I don't know what she thinks.
I want to say she's elegant
and other words I cannot spell
but I just tell her
she stinks.
I want to be nice to her
but I'm horrible instead,
can I have some advice please,
and another slice of bread.

Breakfast poem

This morning I tipped
my cornflakes from the ripped
box, and a few flew onto the table.
Before placing them in the bowl
and spooning them into the usual hole
I drew them.
Of the drawings,
some looked like rocks
some looked like countries
none looked like pajamas
and one looked a little like a dog.
This morning I missed my bus.

What a poem's not

☒ A poem is not an **A**nt
but it can be quite short.

☒ A poem is not a **B**anana
but there may be something under its skin.

☒ A poem is not a **C**oat
but it may have some warmth in it.

☒ A poem is not a **D**og
and it can do without a basket.

☒ A poem is not an **E**ndless pair of pants
but it can be quite long.

☒ A poem is not a **F**ootball
shaped like a cucumber.

☒ A poem is not a **G**oat shaped like
a piece of chewing gum.

☒ A poem is not a **H**edgehog
but it might be hard to get hold of.

☒ A poem is not an **I**diot
but it can be quite stupid.

☒ A poem is not a **J**ack-in-the-box
but it can be quite stupid.

☒ A poem is not a **K**ite
but it might blow away.

☒ A poem is not a **L**ight bulb
but you can change it if you want to.

☒ A poem is not a **M**onkey
but it can be quite human.

40

☒ A poem is not a **N**ut
but you can give it to a monkey.
☒ A poem is not an **O**okookookookookook
ookookookooloombomanumakookoo.
☒ A poem is not a **P**rison
and it shouldn't feel like one either.
☒ A poem is not a **Q**uestion
actually it is sometimes.
☒ A poem is not a **R**adio
but you may have to tune in to it.
☒ A poem is not a **S**cab
so don't pick it.
☒ A poem is not a **T**oothbrush
so don't clean your teeth with it.
☒ A poem is not an **U**mbrella
but it may give protection.
☒ A poem is not a **V**ery big plantar wart
and I'm glad.
☒ A poem is not a **W**ig
but you can wear it if you want to.
☒ A poem is not an **X**-ray
make no bones about it.
☒ A poem is not a **Y**ear-old bag of vegetables
but it can smell quite strongly.
☒ A poem is not a **Z**ylophone
and it can spell words wrongly.

Loaf poem

I bought a loaf the other day
it came to life and ran away.
And I said,
"Naughty bad bread.
NAUGHTY."

**L
E
A
F** poems

Little
Earwigs
And
Fruit

Let's
Eat
A
Fridge

Lions'
Ears
Are
Few

Laughter
Eats
Away
Fear

Large
Elbows
Are
Fantastic

Look
Everyone
A
Fish.

Tree poem

t h e
leaves
h a v e
all left
b u t
t h e
t r e e
will be
a l l
right

Key poem

Being a key
is my curse.
I live on a ring
in a purse
or a pocket
rarely seeing my true home.
Only for a moment,
when I unlock it.

Sea poem

The shallows
the deeps
the blues and
the greens,
the seaweed
and the submarines.
The lifetimes of swimming and no sweat
the lines of yachts
and lots and lots
and lots and lots and lots and lots and
 lots and lots and lots
of wet.

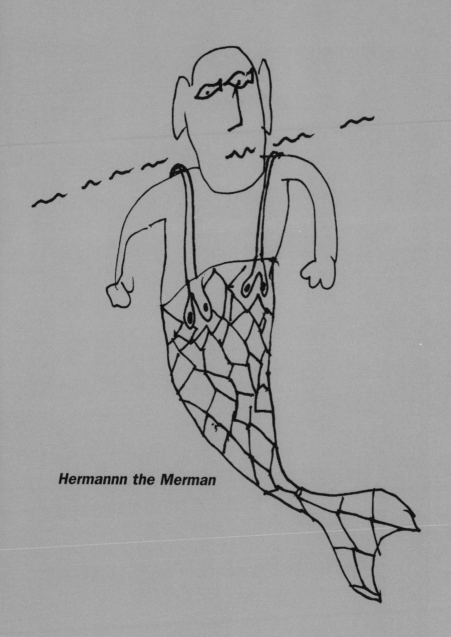

Hermannn the Merman

47

The emergensea

The octopus awoke one morning and wondered

what rhyme it was.

Looking at his alarm-clocktopus

he saw that it had stopped

and it was time to stop having a rest

and get himself dressed.

On every octofoot

he put

an octosocktopus

but in his hurry, one foot got put

not into an octosocktopus

but into an electric outlet

and the octopus got a nasty electric shocktopus

and had to call the octodoctopus

who couldn't get in

to give any help or medicine

because the door was loctopus.

The octopus couldn't move, being in a state of

octoshocktopus

so the octodoctopus bashed the door

to the floor

and the cure was as simple as could be:

a nice refreshing cup of

seawater.

∧ ∧

FLEA POEM

Dog's back.	Scratch.
Itch	itch
itch	paws
scratch	scratch
scratch	scratch
scratch	scratch
scratch	scratch
scratch	scratch
scratch	scratch
pause	
scratch	scratch
	scratch
itch	scratch scratch scratch
scratch	bald patch.

BEE POEM

I'm stripey and I'm wipey

when I'm visiting the flowers

I dust and dive,

my wings sing buzz

for hours

and ours

is a happy old hive.

I live in a colony.

I like to get all polleny.

Cup of tea poem

 Tea

 Tea

 Tea

 Tea

 Empty

Knee poem

Once when I was in a shopping mall
I banged my knee
and went,
"Aah m'knee m'knee!"
And someone gave me
some m'ney.

When the wind is up
you can get the height,
the tail flaps wild
and the sails in flight,
but do remember to
hold on tight, otherwise you might lose your

kite

FREDDIE FOUR LEGS

Hello, I'm Freddie Four Legs,
I've got more legs than you.
I've got more than what is normal legs
and I've got four feet too.
When I'm in a shoe shop
I don't just buy a pair
and when I ride a bicycle,
there's two legs going spare.
But this is not the problem,
it's the people who call out
inflammatory comments
that I complain about.
They just see what is wrong with me
they're just not being fair
they've never seen my brilliant
impression of a chair.

Most days I can take it
but there's times I take it bad
especially when the nasty comments
come from Mom and uncle,
but looking on the brighter side
it does seem so unfair but
while they make fun of my four legs
they overlook my tiny eye,
and my very silly haircut.

Armadillo

my mommy she bought me an armadillo
I kissed him and kept him under my pillow
and I cleaned him with a Brillo pad
he was shiny and tiny and he came from Peru
his name was Armadeus
but we used to call him Toby
he had a suit of armor and he burrowed about
the hills and the daffodils he turned them inside out
and my mother used to shout at him
when he came home covered in graffiti
he was an insectivorous creature
the teacher used to say
and the dog next door
the carnivore
would sometimes come and play
we had races and chases down by the willow
and sometimes we'd go swimming and sometimes
   we wouldn't
he had ants and beetles for dinner every day

them creepy-crawlies he could put 'em away
and he did his indoor doings
in his indoor doings tray
but one day in the winter
when the willow tree was bare
I looked under my pillow
and there was nobody there
I ran downstairs
and I said to my mommy
Mommy where's he gone?
she was having a game of rummy
and she looked up and she said John
go and put some clothing on
you're nearly twenty-four
and I said sorry Mom it's an emergency
and I ran out in the raw
and I ran down to the riverside
and in a rowboat I saw
Toby
in the distance
with the dog next door

JACK iN
the box

FOX iN
the box

BEAR iN the chair

PAIN iN the neck

Neck

We used to have a teacher in our
school whom we called Neck.
We called him Neck because he had
such a long neck.
He also had big sprigs of hair
which came sprouting out of his nose,
but we weren't interested in those.
We were too keen on his neck,
we'd never seen such a neck,
it was a heck of a neck.

neck and neck

My dog is a dog

When I finally got a real dog of my own
of course I was glad
that I was no longer alone
but also, in the end it had
been good to be without such a friend,
as it made me see
the dog in a log
the dog in the TV,
in my tea
in my cornflakes . . .
and of course
in my carrots.
My new dog was great,
and he was worth his wait
in gold
and orange
and many other colors.

Goodbye